ŒLEGY OF THE SOUL

ABHINAV SUNDAR

notionpress.com

INDIA • SINGAPORE • MALAYSIA

Contents

Bygone

A callous crown, a jaded heart,
I built these walls to keep love apart.
A walking wound, a self-made mess,
But in this wreckage, I confess,

A flicker sparked, a yearning deep,
To mend the scars I used to keep.
Then fate, a jester, cruel and sly,
Brought you an angel with a smile so fly.

Godly touch, a gentle gaze,
You saw through cracks in my sorry maze.
You held my hand, a soothing balm,
A quiet strength, a whispered calm.

The jagged edges, worn and torn,
Slowly softened, hope newborn.
But shadows linger, whispers creep,
A chilling fear I quite can't sleep.

A cruel blow, a car's harsh screech,
The world stands still; my voice won't reach.
You lie there pale, with a vacant stare,
The memory thief, burden thou bear.

Days crawl by, a blur of white,
Recovery's glow, a painful sight.
New laughter rings, not meant for me,
A gentle touch, a different plea.

Another hand to hold yours tight,
A stranger's love in dawning light.
You mend, you heal, a happy start,
But my reflection fades from your heart.

I stand unseen, a broken shell,
The one you loved, the fucked up rebel.
No bitter tears, no rage screamed,
Just a hollow silence, a wound unseen.

Green Eyed

They sing of love, a tender flame,
A soaring bliss, a whispered game.
But all I see is burning ash,
A fleeting warmth, all lovers crash.

They clutch and swoon with tearful eyes,
A tangled mess of sweet goodbyes.
A fickle dance, a heart laid bare,
Love's laced beauty with dark despair.

I watch them fall, with envy's sting,
Yet, in my core, no love can sing.
Perhaps I'm cursed, this heart of stone,
Forever lost, forever alone.

The world's a stage, a play of two,
Where lovers find their dreams come true.
But in the wings, unseen, I stand,
A loveless ghost in this love-struck land.

Is this my fate, this barren ground?
No tender touch, no laughter's sound?
To never know love's sweet embrace,
Its whispered hope, its saving grace?

They say it heals, it cuts so deep,
A bittersweet, lovely thing to keep.
I yearn to know this love they sing,
To feel its sting, the joy it brings.

Perchance

The wreckage of my life, a light gone dark,
Each broken piece, a promise I discard.
I built the pyre, ignited by hand,
And watched it burn this sorry, broken land.

The beast within whispers in my ear,
"This happiness, my friend, you'll surely smear.
You're rotten to the core, a blight, a curse,
This love, this life, will all turn worse."

The tears they fall, a salty, stinging rain,
The weight of failure, a suffocating chain.
Ungrateful wretches, a burden on their hearts,
I'll push them all away, tear love apart.

But embers glow, a flicker in the dark,
A fragile hope, a brand new spark.
I pick it up, this ember, warm and small,
And start to mend the wreckage, brick by wall.

This perfect thing, so fragile, built with care,
My clumsy hands will surely leave it, please, don't dare.
The road is so long, the battle yet to wage,
But maybe, just maybe, I can turn this page.

Revival

Beaten and broken and bruised, he scoffs at fate's guests,
In life's twisted game, he stands the test.
Mocking the weaklings who cower and hide,
He sneers at their fears with darkness and pride.

Beaten and broken and bruised, yet he mocks,
The notion of surrender, the act of chains on his name.
With each fucked up day, he still stands bright as day,
For he knows in his heart, fuck it, we rule every day.

Beaten and broken and bruised, he strides in with cheer,
Through life's absurdity, he holds nothing dear.
Scorning the naysayers who tremble and quail,
He revels in the chaos with a triumphant wail.

Beaten and broken and bruised, but never subdued,
He taunts the struggles with badmouthing and booze.
For in life's comedy, he finds his stage,
A raucous performer, taunting rage.

Riposte

A ray of sunshine, that's how she appeared,
A friendship blossomed, a bond I revered.
We laughed, and we shared, secrets whispered in ears,
Best friends forever, erasing all fears.

Something shifted, a flicker in my gaze,
A deeper feeling, caught in love's sweet maze.
But friendship's armour, I dared not to break,
Content with her presence, for her happiness's sake.

The mask she wore, oh, it fooled me so well,
A viper disguised, a story to tell.
Underneath kindness, a heart black as night,
She'd tear me to pieces with cruel, cutting eyes.

Burned and discarded, shattered on the floor,
The girl of my dreams wanted nothing more
Than to watch me crumble, to laugh at my plight,
Then, walk away, leaving me lost in the fight.

The world's a vast canvas, and I'll paint it bright,
Conquer my demons and take back the light.
She may be a villain, a queen of deceit,
But I am the hero, the best of the fucked up, repeat.

Torn, yes I am, by the love and the pain,
Shadows linger through the pouring rain.
For breaking me open exposed all my flaws,
Now stronger and wiser, defying the laws

Of self-doubt and sorrow, I stand tall and proud,
The best version of me, emerging from the cloud.
She may call herself queen, but that's just a mess,
For the king of his castle will always be the best.

Just Hollow

The sugar's lost its sweetness, once a joyful bite,
Now, cardboard in my mouth, a flavourless plight.
The clothes I used to tear hang limp on the wall,
No dress to wear, the hell happened this fall.

The latest tech marvel, a soulless machine,
No thrill in its power, no digital glee.
The books on the shelf, once portals to dreams,
Now pages of dust where no magic gleams.

The silver screen flickers, a monochrome show,
No heroes to cheer for, no villains to loathe.
Life's vibrant colours fade to a grey,
The colours of passion are all withering away.

Is this a cruel joke, a twist of the mind?
The things that once held me now leave me behind.
Is love a fickle flame destined to wane?
Leaving just ashes, a soul filled with pain.

Rekindled?

My heart, a rusted compass, spun in vain,
Lost in a world of grayscale, washed with rain.
A weary traveller, I trudged the beaten path,
Shoulders slumped, a ghost of a forgotten laugh.

Then you, a sunrise, burst upon the scene,
Melting frost with a smile, vibrant and keen.
Your eyes, twin pools of laughter, dared me to see,
The playful boy still slumbering within me.

With a gentle hand, you coaxed him from his hold,
Whispered secrets of joy, stories yet untold.
Suddenly, puddles turned to shimmering delight,
And city streets became a stage for playful flight.

You, my love, are the artist with a brush so bright,
Painting colours onto the canvas of my cruel night.
The boy within awakened, hand in hand,
We skip through life, a love-struck, joyous band.

So thank you, love, for the laughter and the light,
For chasing shadows with a heart so kind.
You brought the boy back, tears of the man unfurled,
And in your eyes, I see a future, a love-filled world.

Atone

Another blunder, a misstep I tread,
This tangled web of my own mistakes I've bred.
A web woven with threads of deceit,
A fucked up fumble, a rhythm incomplete.

The voice in my head, a relentless repeat,
Whispers of darkness, a soul filled with greed.
"You're a lost cause," it taunts, with a venomous sting,
"Just end it all, friend. Why make the world sink?

To a wretch like you, a burden so vast?"
But a flicker of hope, a memory uncovered fast.
A time when I strived, when I learned, and I grew,
A sliver of light, a promise anew.

God, or fate, or whatever you call it, my friend,
I don't ask for forgiveness, this misery I intend
To untangle myself, this burden I'll bear,
To find solace within, a strength to repair.

This is my penance, my burden to hold,
To mend what I shattered, a story untold.
Let the world spin on, with its madness and din,
I'll find my own peace from the chaos within.

Misconstrued

Inked with midnight, a feathered taboo,
The crow takes to flight, a misunderstood boo.
A symbol of omens, of darkness and dread,
But this crow here dreams of a brighter hue spread.

His heart beats with kindness, unseen by the throng,
He longs for a chance to right every wrong.
He gathers lost trinkets, a glint in his eye,
Not treasures for hoarding, but gifts for those nigh.

He watches the farmer, with seeds in his hand,
And scatters a few for the birds in the land.
He warns of the hawk, with a caw sharp and clear,
Protecting the fledglings, dispelling all fear.

He cleans fallen berries, a feast for the ants,
A silent assistance, with gentle, black pants.
His voice, once a portent, now sings a sweet tune,
A melody hopeful beneath the full moon.

The world sees him grim, with judgment so fast,
But this crow holds a spirit, pure and unsurpassed.
He yearns to be known for the good that he does,
Beyond superstition, a friend to all of us.

So listen, dear people, and open your eyes,
For darkness and light, in all creatures, arise.
This crow, misunderstood, with a heart full of grace,
Just wants to be seen for the good in his space.

Shoosh

Foggy thoughts, a constant ache,
World's a blur, a heart that breaks.
Tears may fall like cleansing rain,
Strength will rise to ease the pain.

Damn, I'm fucked,
Damn, it pains.
Oh, shut I know,
No gain from complaints,
Fuck it, we rule every day.

Idiots>>>

9B, a whisper, a name on the door,
But echoes of laughter can't ring anymore.
Shuffled and scattered, like leaves in the fall,
A friendship's warm haven now shattered and small.

Fettle

A broken heart, a mosaic of pain,
Fragments scattered, dreams in disdain.
Yet within the chaos, a legend's tale,
Of resilience and strength that shall prevail.

Piece by piece, she gathers the shards,
Binding them together, creating new guards.
Each crack and crevice, a story to tell,
Of a soul that triumphs through love's farewell.

The mosaic of the heart, a work of art,
Stitched with courage, an extraordinary part.
For legends are woven from shattered dreams,
And broken hearts, reborn at the seams.

Basal

Beneath the smile, the laughter's disguise,
Lies a weariness hidden from prying eyes.
Tired souls yearn to cast away the charade,
To be accepted, embraced, and unafraid.

Pardon

Slipped from my hand, a laugh turned to a scream,
Your eyes, once stars, now a lifeless dream.
Guilt's a shroud, heavy, can't breathe, can't see,
Failed you, my friend, I'm a mockery.

World spins, oblivious, a hollow inside,
Friendship's a lie, where did the light hide?
Darkness whispers, a tempting cat chase,
But your memories flicker, lighting my tear-filled face.

Hand slipped, laugh died in a choked scream,
Your eyes, once bright, a shattered dream.
Guilt's a fist, crushing, can't breathe, can't see,
Just failed you, my friend. So sorry, so sorry, it's me.

Nonsense

Stuck, a fly in amber, life's a film on mute,
Days blur like colours, a world I can't compute.
Laughter and the bright side, a distant, faded dream,
Replaced by shadows, where nothing's what it seems.

The clock ticks onward, a cruel and mocking beat,
While I stand frozen, a ghost on an empty street.
Is this all there is? This cosmic, cosmic joke?
A tangled mess unraveling, with nowhere left to choke.

Aching for meaning, a reason to ignite,
But purpose flickers, a dim and dying light.
The world's a funhouse, mirrors all distort,
Reality's fractured, a twisted, broken court.

So I stand here, broken, a prisoner of time,
Wishing for answers, a purpose, a rhyme.
Lost in the chaos, a world I can't rewind,
Just a whisper, "Maybe meaning is what we leave behind."

Flukes

He struts through town, a devil sinning,
Tail curled with pride, a damn bright grin.
No pitchfork held, no fiery gleam,
Just smiles so wide, a radiant beam.

Forget the flames, the hell hard hold,
This devil's heart, by love, unfolds.
An angel's touch, a whispered sigh,
Melted his ice with a tear in his eye.

Across the void, a stolen glance,
A whispered vow, a fateful chance.
No threats of hell, but moonlit grace,
A world unveiled a hidden space.

He showed her tears and laughter's sound,
The world's soft shades, where joy was found.
Beyond the gate, a love so true,
He defied fate for love anew.

She fell for him with gentle grace,
An angel's heart in his embrace.
He holds her close with joyous glee,
My love's a fire for all to see.

On earthly ground, bathed in sunlight,
A wedding grand, a glorious sight.
His hidden horns, a floral crown,
A devil changed by love's renown.

Fervid

Forget shooting stars, your smile's the light I chase,
Warmth that melts away worries, god damn,
it's love's sweet little race,
You're perfect, flawless, a whimsical rhyme,
And with you, my dear, all me is,
all I can be, is a truly, utterly goofy
little idiot lost in time.

You like shiny things, it's true, my dear,
But could we wed with paper rings, sincere?
For it's not the gold but our love that binds,
Together forever, good hearts intertwined.

You like shiny things, but could
we get married with paper rings?
With you, my love, I would do anything.

Yonder

In the heat of anger, words like swords,
Clash between father and son, in discord.
Each syllable a strike, each silence a wound,
In the battlefield of pride, hearts are marooned.

Egos clash like thunder in the sky,
As the storm of fury brews, high.
Resentment simmers, a tempest brews,
In the clash of wills, both souls refuse.

Maybe tomorrow, I'll find the way,
To mend the bridge, build a brighter day.
To swallow pride, with a whispered plea,
"Forgive my anger, and set me free."

Yay...

My hero's eyes, once filled with pride,
Now hold a flicker, dimmed inside.
He claps for others, pats their backs,
A hollow ache behind his cracks.

Trophies gleam on shelves, not mine,
Just empty spaces, marking time.
His booming laugh, for wins, not mine,
A constant echo, a cruel design.

I clench my fists, a silent rage,
This constant fight on this life's stage.
His expectations, a crushing weight,
I'm just a shadow, sealed by fate.

Maybe greatness skips a beat,
Maybe my path lies down a different street.
But still, it stings, that look of doubt,
A broken promise, a whispered shout.

Maybe someday I'll find my own,
A different mountain, a different throne.
But for now, the silence hangs so thick,
A heavy burden, a broken brick.

Go On, Please

They rant of the end, with a feverish pitch,
While I sip on my tea, with a barely suppressed twitch.
Their words used to sting like a wasp in the night,
Now they're just background buzz with a lacklustre light.

The weight of the world that once bent my spine,
Has faded to whispers, a barely heard whine.
I watch the whole drama unfold on stage,
With a cynical smirk, just a smile on my mind.

Let them scream, let them shout, let the world crawl all over,
I've found a quiet corner, a space to simply travel.
Through worlds spun from fancy, where just Me, Myself and I fight in delight,
I'm no longer a mirror reflecting their petty, stupid plight.

So here's to detachment, a shield from the fray,
A poet who found peace in a world gone astray.
Let the storm rage on, let the cynics all scoff,
I'll just sit back and chuckle with a gentle little laugh.